PRECISELY

Driving Greater Retirement Readiness
through MassMutual PlanALYTICS^{SM}

Contents

Please note that this book uses the term "401(k)" as an easy referent covering a broad range of retirement plans, including 457, 403(b), 401(a), and other plan types.

Foreword

By Fred Barstein

Pick up any newspaper today and you'll see that the retirement program in the United States is at a crossroads. Conflicting articles are printed daily, documenting both the successes and the failures of the system. The industry as a whole gets a black eye from the media, while regulators and lawmakers engage in highly politicized attempts to "fix" the system. It is extremely difficult for the average American to know whether we are declaring victory or calling for an end to the 401(k) as a retirement savings vehicle. With all of that going on, it's important for retirement professionals to have some perspective and understanding of how we got to where we are now, as well as a clear vision of where we need to go.

Precisely: Driving Greater Retirement Readiness through MassMutual PlanALYTICS does both. The book starts with a historical look back at retirement to provide industry professionals with a clear understanding of how the idea of retirement, as well as the ways we plan for it, have evolved into what we know today. With an understanding of where we are now, *Precisely* offers MassMutual's vision of where we're headed.

Retirement was easy when people did not live long enough to enjoy it. Otto von Bismarck was famous for setting the retirement age at sixty-five[1] knowing that, at the time, most people would not live that long. And though the development of defined benefit plans was seen as a panacea along with Social Security, the fundamental problem is about risk: who will bear the risk of people retiring – or worse, unable to work – without having enough money to live? Under 401(k) plans, that risk is squarely with the participants, who now need to determine how much to save, how to invest, and how to make sure they do not outlive their savings.

There are many riddles wrapped up in enigmas that make up present-day 401(k)s. First, today's defined contribution plans don't carry the same guarantees that defined benefit plans did, and saving enough on which to retire is up to the individual. Second, the party making the decisions about setting up and running a company's retirement plan is not carrying the risk of investing. Third, the individual participants who are making the savings decisions in hopes of being prepared for retirement are ill-equipped on at least two major fronts: in addition to their general lack of knowledge about how to save in a way that best suits their needs and lifestyle, they face the additional sabotage of having been programmed by our present-day economy to be spenders, not savers.

Under the weight of all these issues, it's close to a miracle that there are over \$14 trillion in participant-directed defined contribution plans and IRAs, dwarfing the size of defined benefit plans as well as state and municipal plans. And yet, despite the challenges they face, 401(k)s are alive and well.

---

[1] Although it isn't really true. The retirement age was initially set at seventy, when Bismarck was seventy-four. It wasn't until eighteen years after he died that the retirement age was lowered to sixty-five. http://www.ssa.gov/history/ottob.html

Precisely lays out very practical ways that advisors, plan sponsors, and participants can overcome the inherent challenges we face in saving for retirement and find good reason to have hope for the future.

By blending behavioral finance with the power of big data and persona-based marketing, the retirement industry has at its disposal the tools required to shift the paradigm. And a paradigm shift is what's needed. Think of the advent and evolution of the automobile. Things kicked off with Ford's imperfect and clunky Model T, which wasn't pretty but got the user from A to B. Since then, science, engineering, and consumer needs and expectations have evolved, and the paradigm is shifting as we head toward Tesla's electronic cars, a vast improvement on the original automobiles. They're both cars, but each one speaks to the needs of its times.

Precisely posits that the 401(k) is the right tool for the future, but – like the Tesla – it must be upgraded with a focus on precision and ease. For the 401(k) industry to get there, we must be focused on outcomes, which we need to measure not company by company but person by person. A pioneer in plan health, MassMutual is taking the next step forward with PlanALYTICS and the various tools they have developed to not only measure success but also to improve its chances through the use of big data and technology, resulting in customized plans and communication campaigns. Our industry's future, according to MassMutual, may be in moving toward the day when an employer gives their workers a set amount of money to spend on a variety of benefits from which they can choose depending on their needs and situation. Obviously, in order for individual savers to get into the driver's seat when it comes to their retirement and benefits, they need to know what they're doing – so we have to go beyond trying to predict what they might need based on data and get them engaged as active participants in planning for their future – even when auto features are being employed.

With greatly expanded life expectancies that seem to grow exponentially, technology that never seems to stop amazing us, and a quality of life surpassing what any past generation has ever known, retirement now means financial freedom rather than not working. How do we as industry professionals provide more participants with a greater chance for success while satisfying employers' needs to run their businesses profitably? While there is no silver bullet, MassMutual has clearly laid out the problem and has offered some interesting and practical solutions putting themselves, clients, and partners ahead of the pack as an industry thought leader.

Precisely: Driving Greater Retirement Readiness through MassMutual PlanALYTICS is a must-read for the thoughtful and passionate retirement professional.

Acknowledgements

*"A group of people get together and exist as an institution
we call a company so they are able to accomplish
something collectively that they could not accomplish
separately – they make a contribution to society, a
phrase which sounds trite but is fundamental."*

– David Packard, co-founder of Hewlett-Packard

This book is authored by and represents the collective thinking and work of approximately 2,500 MassMutual Retirement Services and Worksite Insurance employees. With that said, the book did not write itself. While many dedicated employees contributed, we want to acknowledge and thank Leila Martin as the creative force who pulled the content together in a format that has made it a delight to read. In addition, we thank Heather Smiley for her vision in recognizing the need for a book that documents this type of thought leadership. Thank you, as well, to the following individuals without whose contributions and support this book would not have been written:

Steve Jackson	Sara Wolk	James Viola
Tina Wilson	Michelle Morey	Elaine Sarsynski
Jill O'Brien	Camille Donald	Kris Gates
Nick Morris	Wally Swist	

Introduction:

A Roadmap to Retirement Happiness

It's understandable that today's pre-retirees, many
of them Baby Boomers[2] who didn't save as much as they
should have, are nervous about what will happen with their
money in retirement. We know that Boomers have the larg-
est retirement savings gap of all the generations, and the
most challenging prognosis for addressing it. Many people
close to retirement see their savings gap and plan to rely on
the solution of working longer. However, we also know that
45% of current retirees retired earlier than they had planned,
primarily due to reasons beyond their immediate control.
So working longer isn't necessarily a reliable option. Which
begs the question: just how bad is the "retirement crisis"
that these folks are experiencing today?

In order to answer that question, MassMutual com-
missioned a body of research on pre-retirees and retirees.
The study, entitled "Hopes, Fears and Reality – What
Workers Expect in Retirement and What Steps Help Them
Achieve the Retirement They Want," surveyed more than
1,800 people, all of whom fell somewhere on the spectrum
between being fifteen years away from retirement to being
fifteen years into it. Of the retirees, six in ten reported being
"very satisfied with their retirement lifestyle,"[3] and most of
them recounted a general increase of positive emotions with
a general decrease of negative emotions once in retirement.
Retirees, for example, are:

[2] Those born between mid-1946 and 1964. US Census Bureau, "The Older Population:
2010," US Census Bureau, November 2011, page 4. http://www.census.gov/prod/
cen2010/briefs/c2010br-09.pdf
[3] "Hopes, Fears and Reality – What Workers Expect in Retirement and What Steps Help
Them Achieve the Retirement They Want," Greenwald & Associates on behalf of Mass-
Mutual. (Henceforth referenced as Greenwald, "Hopes, Fears and Reality")

happier and more relaxed than pre-retirees. Around 7 in 10 retirees report being extremely happy and extremely relaxed (72% and 67% respectively). In comparison, only 6 in 10 pre-retirees feel extremely happy and only a third feel extremely relaxed (61% and 34%, respectively) [...]. Retirees are also, predictably, less stressed. Forty-three percent of pre-retirees report being at least moderately stressed. Amongst retirees, only 17% report a similar stress level.[4]

The experiences of today's satisfied retirees offer a blueprint for how the generations that follow them – especially the Boomers close to retirement, but also anyone else who hasn't started saving yet – can achieve their best chance at a positive retirement experience. Of all the retirees, eight in ten indicated enjoying themselves and having more free time, and around seven in ten retirees say they have been able to afford a comfortable lifestyle.

In fact, the study unearthed what one might call the "prescription for retirement happiness"[5] by comparing the retirement preparation behaviors of the happiest retirees to those of the least happy retirees. Ten behaviors stood out as driving retirement happiness most strongly:

1. Calculating the best time to begin collecting Social Security benefits

[4] Greenwald, "Hopes, Fears and Reality"
[5] Jennie Phipps, "7 Steps to Retirement Happiness," Bankrate, December 15, 2014, http://www.bankrate.com/financing/retirement/7-steps-to-retirement-happiness/

2. Calculating a target for money needed in order to afford to retire

3. Estimating medical and dental expenses in retirement

4. Working with a financial advisor

5. Creating a budget for retirement

6. Making efforts to increase savings

7. Rebalancing stocks and bonds

8. Making new friends/reconnecting with old friends

9. Focusing on their relationship with spouse or partner

10. Creating a written financial plan for retirement

Among the greatest lessons the surveyed group had to offer was this: don't wait to start planning. Many of those surveyed had to retire earlier than expected, so it was important to them to not delay taking steps to prepare for retirement, since it might come earlier than you think.

When asked, many of those surveyed said they wished they would have saved more (20%) and prepared better financially (17%).[6] However, the study's focus groups brought to light the finding that retirees can be happy in retirement despite not having a perfect financial plan going in. One of the major things to remember about happiness in retirement, according to the AARP, is that "Experiences, not things, enrich your life," and that "If you look back at your past spending, chances are you'll remember fondly — and

[5] Ibid.

perhaps in great detail — experiences you had, as opposed to stuff you bought."[7]

Retired survey participants gave credence to that stance with advice that was not financial but social in nature. "Don't neglect," the research says, "to prepare for the social aspects of retirement such as strengthening the relationship with one's spouse/significant other, cultivating new friendships, and fostering old friendships. The earlier people can make it a priority to focus on the relationship with their spouse or significant other, the better."[8] This advice for social and emotional preparation for retirement is compelling, because the human experience is about so much more than money, and while money is important for retirement, a little human adaptability can go a long way. One of the survey focus groups' conversations points to a wonderful example of this.

A Boston focus group of surveyed retirees referred to the topic, of course, of spending money in retirement. One person stated, "We have to watch what we spend. We can't do a lot of stuff, a lot of traveling, a lot of vacations or anything like that."[9] Another member of the focus group mentioned that he and his wife saw an ad for a Broadway show they really wanted to go see in New York – until they thought about the price tag: "$300 or $400 a night for the hotel. Amtrak is going to be $200 or $300 to go back and forth. You add the whole thing up [and] you're talking $800 - $900 - $1,000. I said, 'I really would like to see that play, but I don't think that's going to happen.' It's just not worth

[7] "5 Financial Secrets to a Happy Retirement," Lynnette Khalifani-Cox, AARP, http://www.aarp.org/work/retirement-planning/info-11-2010/khalfani_cox_secrets_to_happy_retirement.2.html

[8] Greenwald, "Hopes, Fears and Reality"

[9] Greenwald, "Hopes, Fears and Reality" focus group research (unpublished, anonymous participants)

spending that kind of money."[10] And of course, watching what you spend is important in retirement, but that doesn't mean you can't do things you'd spent your entire working life thinking you'd be able to swing once you hit retirement. It just takes a little adapting.

The conversation went on, and a woman in the group offered a brilliant solution for the frustrated theater lovers. "I get to see plays free because I usher […] there's some of these places that if you do office work for them you might get tickets free,"[11] while another group member mentioned that he and his wife used to belong to and sponsor their local theater group, and were able to get discounted tickets to see high-quality shows for a fraction of the cost and with very little travel. Another woman in the group summed it up beautifully, as a discussion of:

> how [to] approach retirement without spending as much money. [There are] all sorts of things that I'm finding out now are free or that I [can] go and get discount tickets for or volunteer for. I think that's the theme that I'm hearing around the table of a way to approach retirement and really [more] realistically figure out, "I'm not going to spend $1,000 to go to New York for that play. Instead I'll do this, this, and this." I think that's kind of how [my husband] and I have approached our retirement.[12]

[10] Ibid.
[11] Ibid.
[12] Ibid.

These discussions show that with a little adaptability and creativity, retirees are finding ways to enjoy their retirement without compromising on the kinds of things they want to do, and without having to spend a ton of money on their adventures. It also highlights the importance of keeping your social and emotional connections and friendships viable and active – in just a few minutes of discussion, these people were able to share post-retirement solutions for saving money while having fun, and this kind of discussion and collaboration can be just as valuable a resource as adaptability in helping retirees to create the retirement that's best suited to balance and work with their wants, interests, lifestyle, and budget.

To understand the position we're in with regard to retirement today, let's take a brief look at the history of retirement in America.

Chapter 1:

A Quick Drive Down Memory Lane

Retirement, in one form or another, has what might be a surprisingly long history in America. Though not widespread, actual provisions for retirement did exist for some early Americans. A 1636 law enacted in Plymouth, Massachusetts provided pensions to men disabled in the course of defending their colonies.[13]

We all know the story from there, more or less. Retirement received a designated age from German Emperor William the First[14] and Chancellor Otto von Bismarck. The rise of industry in America (1876–1900)[15] meant a whole new way to work, but "retirement" still basically meant moving in with the grandchildren and helping out where one could. Something closer to our modern idea of retirement started with pensions, offered in an effort to ease the transition of less productive and older employees out of the labor force, opening the way for younger, more productive workers. Government involvement in pension provision was formalized in 1935 with the enactment of Social Security,[16] which is still a primary source for retirement income for most retirees today. Eventually, the Employee Retirement Income Securities Act (ERISA)[17] came into being, designed

[13] US Department of Veterans Affairs, "VA History in Brief," http://www.va.gov/opa/publications/archives/docs/history_in_brief.pdf

[14] Official Social Security Website, http://ssa.gov/history/age65.html

[15] Library of Congress, http://www.loc.gov/teachers/classroommaterials/presentationsandactivities/presentations/timeline/riseind/

[16] Ibid.

[17] Definition from http://www.dol.gov/ebsa/faqs/faq_compliance_pension.html: The Employee Retirement Income Security Act or ERISA is a Federal law that sets standards of protection for individuals in most voluntarily established, private-sector retirement plans. ERISA requires plans to provide participants with plan information, including important facts about plan features and funding; sets minimum standards for participation, vesting, benefit accrual, and funding; provides fiduciary responsibilities for those who manage and control plan assets; requires plans to establish a claims and appeals process for participants to get benefits from their plans; gives participants the right to sue for benefits and breaches of fiduciary duty; and if a defined benefit plan is terminated, guarantees payment of certain benefits through a Federally chartered corporation, the Pension Benefit Guaranty Corporation (PBGC).

to establish protection that previously hadn't existed for individuals in most voluntarily established, private-sector retirement savings plans.

There is a vision that grew out of the industrial era of retirement as an event: this week you've worked forty hours, next week you'll work zero, here's your gold watch and firm handshake, drinks all around. Although it's less than one hundred years old, this already seems to be the classic vision of retirement. This dichotomy between expectations and reality can lead to a tight spot, especially for the post-World War II generation. The Baby Boomers grew up in the era of defined benefit plans, which guaranteed a steady retirement income in the form of a pension. That kind of retirement is what the Boomers' upbringing prepared them for,[18] but it's not the reality they face today.

Things have changed a great deal over time, and living well into one's nineties is a distinct possibility. With modern medicine and generally healthier lifestyles prevailing, Boomers are looking at living longer than ever, and despite the pension-based world they grew up in, these days they have to own their own retirement planning, making sure they're committed to saving enough for a retirement that could stretch decades past the point when they stop working.

A sound retirement is not a pipe dream – but it's a goal that takes a solid strategy to achieve, and in today's world of disappearing pensions, each American is held more and more individually responsible for building and executing that strategy.

---

[18] Mercer, "It's time to Rise to the Retirement Challenge," 2013, http://www.mercer.com/content/mercer/global/all/en/insights/point/2014/mercer-stanford-center-on-longevity-main.html

Is it difficult? Undeniably. Is it possible to mitigate the effects? Yes. With planning, understanding, and a firm grasp of reasonable expectations, a retirement on one's own terms is still completely attainable. It can get a little complicated, sure, but it makes the question for our industry exceedingly simple: how can we best help individuals bear the burden of figuring out how to maximize their own retirement?

Chapter 2:

Why Are We Talking About Cars?

*"The motor car is, more than any other object, the expression
of the nation's character and the nation's dream."[19]*

The Importance of Measurement

Human needs span the gamut from the very basic – food
and shelter – to the very complex, like a feeling of belonging
and knowing where we stand within our social structure, or
constructing our days around our shared concept of time.
The more complex needs all seem to have something in
common, and stand as examples of one of the most significant, fundamental elements in our lives: *measurement*.

We measure *everything*. We measure ourselves to be able
to appropriately purchase clothes and shoes; we measure
time to keep our days structured and organized; we measure
to design the most technologically advanced automobiles;
and we can also use measurement to find or create the most
pertinent retirement program to serve us and our families.

Let's dwell, for a minute, on the automobiles.

In 1913, the Model T was a wonder of technology not
only in what it was, but in how it came to be. Henry Ford,
after all, changed the face of the automotive industry with
sequential manufacturing that used machine tools and fix-
tures specially designed and systematically arranged along
his assembly lines.[20] Before Ford, there was no real mass
production in the automotive world; cars were made by
hand, piece by piece, in a stationary workshop. Advances in
metal stamping and machine equipment, new (at the time)

[19] E. B. White, "Motor Cars," *One Man's Meat*, Trinity House, 1938
[20] http://en.wikipedia.org/wiki/Mass_production

technologies like all-steel bodies and shock absorbers, and a ready supply of willing workers made the Model T happen along the banks of the Detroit River. However, there were issues, as there tend to be with anything in the early stages of its development. In his article, "From Hand Cranking to Charging: Why Tesla's Model S Is the Model of Our Time," Bill Roberson states that "Once started (never easy), the Model T is almost hysterically complicated and dangerous to pilot. Drivers need to watch where they are going while simultaneously doing the hand jive and tap dancing. It makes cell-chatting teen drivers look like paragons of focused, safe driving."[21] He compares this to the Tesla Model S of today. "Walk up to it," Roberson writes,

> and the door handles emerge from their flush position in anticipation of your arrival. Sit down in the sculpted seats and a giant 17-inch vertical touch screen in the center of the dash beckons with maps, endless settings, energy reports, ride controls, cellular-based Internet, a backup camera and more, all in split screen if you'd like. There are no keys to turn, no button to push to start it up. Step on the brake and the elegant driver's display spools up quickly, then pull the little lever by the wheel to "D," and the Tesla Model S is ready to drive. No warming up. No shift linkage. No drama. [...] It's just impressive from any angle, both visually and of course, technologically.[22]

[21] Bill Roberson, "From Hand Cranking to Charging: Why Tesla's Model S Is the Model of Our Time," *Digital Trends*.
September 14, 2013. www.digitaltrends.com/cars/automotive-revolutions-100-years-apart-how-the-past-predicts-the-future-of-driving/
[22] Ibid.

Roberson's appreciation of the precision-engineered Tesla Model S is much on the same level as one might associate with the fit of a luxury leather glove on the hand or a bespoke shoe on the foot. "A glass-smooth electric motor the size of a big watermelon sits spinning between the rear wheels, propelling nearly two and half tons of weight with a single gear and over 400 horsepower. There is no throb of the engine in the steering wheel, no low-level buzz through any surface in the car. Talk normally. Enjoy the ride—just buckle up and hold on."[23]

The message here is one of ease, especially when compared with the Model T experience – in short, just get in and drive. The vision of something better, paired with and supported by data, technology, and measurement, has come together to inform the precision engineering that has taken the automobile to new heights of safety, comfort, and usability, culminating (so far) in the Tesla of today. This long line of innovations was paralleled – and helped along – by new ways of measuring to ensure quality and reliability. One hundred years ago automobiles were nonexistent. Today, they're an ever-improving part of daily life across America and the world.

But why discuss automobiles in a book about retirement plans? The answer is right there in the parallels, in the pattern of growth and improvement through innovation and effective measurement.

The original concept of defined contribution plans can be thought of as the Model T of the retirement world: they answered the call of their times and transformed retirement by creating a vehicle for personal savings and revolution-ized the way people save for, and think about, retirement. But as with the early version of anything brand-new, the first cars and the first retirement plans were clunky and not necessarily easy to drive. But time goes on, and the design improves as it is based more and more on measurement, precision, and specific data.

That combination allows for an electrifying marriage of precision and action. The engineering of the Tesla Model S – driven by data, precision, and measurement – is pushing a paradigm shift in the transportation industry. And what the Tesla Model S is doing for cars, MassMutual PlanALYTICS is doing for retirement. The PlanALYTICS philosophy uses complex data and simulations to drive precision engineer-ing behind the scenes, transforming the world of retirement plans just as much as modern electric cars like the Tesla are transforming the transportation industry.

Effective measurement of the right data allows Mass-Mutual to get a detailed look at plan specifics, so the solu-tions we offer based on that data are precision-engineered to the specific needs of each client. The paradigm shift has started. There's a lot of analysis going on behind the scenes, but the engine runs quietly; when it comes to the users, whether they're plan sponsors or plan participants, all they have to do is "get in and drive."

Chapter 3:

Check Your Gauge – It's All About the Savings Rate

It has been said, most notably in the October 2009 issue of *Time* Magazine, that the 401(k) plan is failing.[24] Is it true? David Wray of the Plan Sponsor Council of America points out that comparing 401(k) values "at market peaks with market bottoms is ridiculous"[25] and argues that the *Time* article and others like it

> continually refer to average account balance size, failing to point out the typical 401(k) participant has only eight or nine years of participation with their current employer. They don't mention the hundreds of billions of dollars rolled over from 401(k)s into IRAs every year. They don't report that 401(k) participants have 15 million accounts worth hundreds of billions of dollars with former employers. [They] use extreme market points to evaluate 401(k) performance [and] fail to report that employer contributions, dollar cost averaging, and market returns over time make 401(k) plans the safest place in America to save.[26]

Part of the tension may be in the contrast between the model of the employer-provided pension and the model of the 401(k) retirement savings plan.

---

[24] Steve Gandel, Time Magazine, "Why It's Time to Retire the 401(k)," http://content.time.com/time/magazine/article/0,9171,1929233,00.html

[25] David Wray, Plan Sponsor Council of America, "Time Magazine 401(k) Article; Advocacy Dressed Up in Journalism," 10/13/2009, http://www.psca.org/time-magazine-401-k-article-advocacy-dressed-up-in-journalism

[26] Ibid.

Although employer-provided, defined benefit pensions are by and large no longer offered to employees, that model has been a powerful shaper of the American idea of retirement for a long time. Because of this, America still faces some "growing pains" when it comes to individuals saving on their own in a 401(k), 403(b), IRA, or other retirement savings plan. And there are dialogues, like the one between *Time* Magazine and the PSCA, that pit defined contribution plans against an expansion of Social Security benefits, trying to figure out the best way to "save" the future of retirement.

But what seems to be the real crux of the matter is not that the defined contribution system doesn't work, because it does – the problem is that people aren't using it correctly, i.e., they just aren't saving enough. "Most of the problem," one argument states,

> in 401(k)s and public sector pension plans
> [...] stems from the fact that companies and
> individuals simply weren't saving enough.
> If most people were putting 15–20% of
> their income into savings, they would be
> fine. But most people weren't. They were
> putting in 4%. Or 0%. To this day, when I
> tell people that they need to save 15% of
> their income, I am greeted with the same
> sort of disbelief that might greet a sugges-
> tion that they move to Tanzania and become
> big-game hunters.[27]

[27] Megan McArdle, "Sorry, Folks: One Way or the Other, You'll Never Be Able to Complete-ly Count on Retirement," The Daily Beast, March 15, 2013. http://www.thedailybeast.com/articles/2013/03/15/sorry-folks-one-way-or-the-other-you-ll-never-be-able-to-count-on-retirement.html

Somewhere, people seem to have gotten the idea that if they start tucking away maybe five or eight percent of their income somewhere in their late thirties or early forties, it'll be easy sailing in retirement. It's no wonder that some cry "failure," but the problem isn't in the system – it's in the people who don't maximize their use of it, if they elect to use it at all.

Now, if you asked the average person whether they think they *should* be enrolled in and contributing to their employer's retirement plan, the answer will likely fall in the spectrum between "yes" and "probably." People in general seem to know they should be saving. So why don't they?

People are stymied by some combination of four things: either they're getting messaging that's confusing or overwhelming; they're just plain procrastinating, because it's easier not to deviate from the status quo; they're reluctant, because they don't want you to tell them they need to give up something they love, like the ritual of their daily afternoon latte, in order to have a shot at retiring with adequate replacement income. Or, on an even simpler level, they might just be overwhelmed and not sure where to start. So even in an environment where people know they *should* save, not as many actually *do*.

The challenge for retirement providers, then, is this: in order to help more Americans save appropriately for retirement, the messaging they get needs to be clear, relevant, timely, and actionable. After all, the Ford Model T worked in the sense that it would get a person from A to B, but it was a clunky experience, the vehicle "[s]pindly, loud, smelly, oily, smoky, unreliable and complicated to operate."[28]

But when it comes to the clients' experience, it should be smooth, clean, and as easy as possible; they shouldn't have to worry about the engineering behind it. They should be able to just get in and drive.

[28] http://www.digitaltrends.com/cars/automotive-revolutions-100-years-apart-how-the-past-predicts-the-future-of-driving/

Chapter 4:

The Retirement Assembly Line

So how does it work? How do you put together the pre-cision engine that drives better retirement outcomes? The key is in the combination of understanding people through the effective use of big data, a grasp of behavioral finance, and persona-based marketing strategies.

Big Data and the Three-Stage Observation Model

What is Big Data? It's "data sets, typically consisting of billions or trillions of records, that are so vast and complex that they require new and powerful computational resources to process."[29] It sounds complicated, but it's part of our everyday life in this technologically driven world. Every app we download, every purchase we make online, everything we post or like or share on social media, almost everything we do involves us providing information that is then stored, studied, and used to bring us a more personalized user experience. In fact, to grasp why Big Data is such a game-changer, it's important to understand a little bit about the evolution of observation as it relates to data collection. There are three stages of analytics within the data-observation model: descriptive, predictive, and prescriptive.

The "hindsight" stage, descriptive analytics, is the origi-nal purpose of data analytics, and its business is in looking at the past. Things like fund fact sheets or performance fall under this category; static, past information is presented in a purely "here is what happened" capacity. The rear-view data might be used to make decisions – such as choosing which funds to invest in based on past performance – but as always, past performance is no guarantee of future results.

Predictive analytics, the next step in the evolution, is where "insight" comes in – not just looking at the data but finding trends in it. It "involves combing through past information to derive models and analyses that help project future outcomes. The goal is to learn from past mistakes and successes in order to know what to change and what to replicate."[30] This reading of the likely future – or "foresight" – through the insight of predictive analytics leads to the final form, prescriptive analytics, in which data-collectors aren't just predicting outcomes; they're making recommendations based on those data-driven predictions.

Predictive analytics allows businesses to identify patterns in customers' buying habits and, presumably, their needs. Prescriptive analytics drives businesses from observation to action. A perfect example of this kind of data use in action happened at Target Stores.

Marketers at Target Stores started with knowing the power of habit; they also know that there are certain times – generally around major life events like graduating college, getting a new job, buying a house, or having a baby – during which habits are more easily broken and reformed.[31] Birth records, for example, are public, so once a birth is known a woman gets all kinds of offers – but Target wanted to get its foot in the door ahead of the curve and start marketing to pregnant women long before the babies were actually born. With that goal in mind, Target's Guest Marketing Analytics

[30] Chad Brooks, "What is Predictive Analytics?" http://www.businessnewsdaily.com/4938-predictive-analytics.html

[31] Charles Duhigg, *New York Times*, "How Companies Learn Your Secrets," Feb. 2012, http://www.nytimes.com/2012/02/19/magazine/shopping-habits.html?pagewanted=6&_r=2&hp&

team combined the three levels of analytics and were able to identify "about 25 products that, when analyzed together, allowed [the team] to assign each shopper a 'pregnancy prediction' score [and] estimate [a woman's] due date to within a small window."[32]

This, of course, is where prescriptive analytics – recommending a course of action based on given information – kicks in. With this information and insight in hand, Target gained the ability "to send coupons timed to very specific stages of [a woman's] pregnancy."[33] And if a woman starts to form a habit of shopping at Target for things like maternity clothes, bottles, diapers, and other baby-related items, it's only a matter of time before she, a frazzled new parent who may be too tired to go to more than one store, can find all her shopping needs met at Target. This is just one example of how the foresight of prescriptive analytics can be a powerful tool.

When used efficiently and with a purpose, Big Data can improve predictability in product purchase trends and participant behaviors regarding banking transactions, as well as the analysis of plan participants' psychographics.[34] In short, if the bull's-eye of the target for the retirement industry is to improve the retirement readiness of plan participants, Big Data puts a homing device on the arrow.[35]

---

[32] Ibid.

[33] Ibid.

[34] *psychographics*: the marketing and statistical research that distills the classification of often disparate population groups in direct relationship to various psychological data— such as attitudes, concerns, and integrity of individual predilections—that would then offer discernible trends. See also: http://www.merriam-webster.com/dictionary/psy-chographics.

[35] Altaf Darzi, "Big Data: Time for the data to drive the opportunities in the Retirement Industry," Congruent Solutions, 2013. http://coreretirementsolutions.com/big-data-time-for-the-data-to-drive-the-opportunities-inthe-retirement-industry/

The Basics of Behavioral Finance

Big Data is an amazing tool, but when you're dealing with people, you have to take the actual people into account, too. That's where behavioral finance comes in. The employer-offered defined contribution plan is crucial as a vehicle with the potential to help employees save so much more than they would if they were trying to save on their own, but even with a company with a retirement plan in place, there are still challenges. An employer trying to get employees to save more faces three main issues, covered in detail by Shlomo Benartzi and Roger Lewin in *Save More Tomorrow*,[36] a landmark work on behavioral finance as it relates to the retirement savings world. These issues are, in a nutshell, inertia, myopia, and loss aversion.

Inertia is the idea that a body not in motion tends to stay not in motion – people don't typically engage in behaviors that fall outside their everyday status quo, even if they're made to see how beneficial the behavior could be, because we "dislike change and cling to the familiar [and] we especially dislike change if it involves physical or mental effort."[37] Benartzi and Lewin offer the examples of starting a new diet or exercise program – many people swear up and down that they're going to make that change; few ever follow through, despite knowing that better eating or exercising would be in their best interests. Inertia swamps good intentions most of the time – a powerful thing to keep in mind when you're trying to get people to change their habits, because habits are tough to break. Habits are built through a three-step process

---

[36] Shlomo Benartzi with Roger Lewin, *Save More Tomorrow: Practical Behavioral Finance Solutions to Improve 401(k) Plans*, Portfolio/Penguin, 2012.
[37] Ibid.

of cue, routine, and reward:[38] that is, the trigger that initiates the behavior, the behavior itself, and the reward for engaging in that behavior. Habits, then, feed into inertia because people are more likely to stick with the cues and rewards they know, rather than willingly taking on the mental work that's required to break a habit and, in turn, break free of that inertia. The formidable power of inertia is the fact that at the end of the day, it's just easier to stay put.

Myopia, or nearsightedness – in this case, in the temporal sense – is another of the three challenges that gets in the way of adequate retirement planning. There are two parts to this myopia: our tendency to focus on immediate gratification and the now, and also our inability to connect with our future selves. "People," Benartzi and Lewin tell us, "have a strong tendency to focus inordinately on the immediate present, and cannot readily bring into mental focus the distant future [...] Being myopic in the context of saving for retirement [can lead to] serious consequences [as] we blunder our way into decisions that are detrimental to our future financial well-being."[39] It's not just our focus on dealing with the immediate demands of the present that drives this myopia; the other force in play is the identity gap[40] – the very real disconnect between the current self and the future self:

> Psychologists have known for a long time
> that young people do not readily identify
> with their own future selves, for example,

[38] Leslie Brokaw, MIT Sloan Management Review, "Are Habits More Powerful Than Decisions? Marketers Hope So." http://sloanreview.mit.edu/article/are-habits-more-powerful-than-decisions-marketers-hope-so/
[39] Shlomo Benartzi with Roger Lewin, *Save More Tomorrow: Practical Behavioral Finance Solutions to Improve 401(k) Plans*, Portfolio/Penguin, 2012.
[40] Ibid.

a thirty-year-old thinking about someone at
the age of sixty-five and entering retirement.
In the extreme, that future self can seem
like a stranger, someone for whom we
would be unwilling to make sacrifices now.[41]

This mentality isn't that hard to understand – how often does anyone (outside the retirement industry, anyway) really think about what kind of life they'll want to live in some distant future, or how they're going to make that happen, when there are bills to pay and children to raise and jobs to do right here and now?

The third problem at the table is that of loss aversion, or the powerful negative response to loss. This may be the most obvious of the three – who can really say that they look forward to loss on an emotional level, even if they're aware of the fact, as in the case of financial portfolios, that fluctuations are normal and loss is probably not permanent? Loss aversion and myopia work hand in hand, especially when it comes to something like quarterly retirement account statements. Benartzi and Lewin outline an argument wherein quarterly statements, because of their focus on short-term returns, can turn investors into poster children for myopic investing because they're being encouraged to react to the short-term behavior of their investments, even when that behavior is not likely to be an adequate picture of the investment's longer-term performance. The perception of loss and the focus on now drown out the voice of reason reminding us that investments are long-haul interests.

[41] Ibid.

Putting the Person Back in "Persona"

In the past, marketing was conducted largely under the aegis of the "spray and pray" philosophy: create one piece and send it to everyone in the hopes that people will notice and take action. This is like flying a plane with a trailing ad banner over a packed beach and keeping your fingers crossed that someone will respond to it. But this doesn't work very well. Inertia is part of it, but what it really comes down to is competition. At the beach, who's got time to look at your banner when there are umbrellas to set up, waves to play in, and ice creams to buy? And even if they do look, you're just one of many things vying for their attention. Do you think they're going to remember your ad after a day in the sun playing with the kids or catching up on the latest bestseller?

Probably not. We're living in an age of information and advertisement overload. When you turn on the television, you see ads. Take a plane somewhere? You'll see ads all over the airport. Surf the Web? Ads galore. If you love to read on a device like a Kindle, unless you pay a fee or contact Amazon support to have them turned off,[42] there are ads on your screen all the time, pulling your eyes away from your book. And when you pull yogurt out of your fridge and the packaging screams from a red starburst that it has MORE CALCIUM THAN THE LEADING BRANDS!, that's an ad, too.

People are exposed to potentially thousands of ads every day. Of course, many of them are static or passive, so the brain doesn't get totally overwhelmed, but almost

---

[42] Amit Agarwal, Digital Inspiration, " How to Remove Ads from Your Kindle Without Any Hacks," www.labnol.org/software/remove-kindle-ads/28341/

everywhere you look, someone is trying to sell you something. Think, for a minute, about the ads you see every day – whether they appear on your yogurt or your television, your social media feed, your junk mail, the billboards you pass on your commute, or the dealership sticker on the car in front of you. Of all those ads you might see or hear in a given day, how many of them do you remember? And of those you remember, how many do you actually act on and buy the product or service on offer? There are a lot of talented, convincing voices out there trying to get people to do something with their money.

Retirement providers, too – plan sponsors, plan advisors, and marketers alike – comprise one set of the voices trying to get consumers to take action with their money. In our case, of course, we want them to save it, rather than spend it, so our voice is up against a lot of competition. And the competition is not, as some might think, against a bank or another provider. It's against retail giants; companies, like Apple and Target, that are phenomenal at getting the consumer, through targeted advertising, to spend their money – the very same money *we* are trying to get them to *save*. In order to have a shot at beating out savvy retail marketing campaigns, it's necessary to take a page from their book. How are those companies so good at getting people to fork over those hard-earned dollars?

One word: *customization*. When retailers are on their game, the contents of the ads they send you are based on your spending habits. If you buy diapers at a big-box retailer, for example, they're likely to consistently send you coupons for baby stuff – they make a point to learn what you shop for, and they make it easy to keep coming back.

Now consider this: if you buy diapers from a big-box store and they start sending you coupons for auto supplies, would you be likely to go back, or would you be put off and start to wonder whether the store really knew you at all?

The same thing goes for retirement plans. One of the keys to getting employees to save for retirement is *segmentation*, which allows us to tailor our message to, and get the attention of, the recipient. Rather than sticking to "one size fits all" when that's definitely not the case, our marketing and education materials are based on personas, which start with age segmentation and split again based on gender. Then, they're paired with one of four "next best steps," all of which are informed by the data we have on the plan and its participants. The "next best steps" are the four actions possible for participants to take:

1. to sign up and participate in the plan, if they haven't already;

2. to save more, if they're not on track to meet their retirement goals;

3. to review and change how they're allocating assets to get a better mix for them; and

4. to consolidate, if they've got multiple retirement plans floating around with different providers.

On top of that information is another layer – delivery preference. As long as we have the data on file, we'll know whether a participant prefers to get communications through e-mail or through postal mail, and will honor those preferences when materials are sent out. Variation on personas, gender, next best step, and delivery preference create ninety-six distinct personas within the MassMutual system, each one tailored to take the best possible advantage of a person's preferences and make it easy for them to take the necessary steps toward retirement readiness.

This structure is what MassMutual currently uses for its award-winning annual RetireSmart[SM] national campaign.[43] Under this form of segmentation, Sally Jones, a twenty-eight-year-old female, will receive messaging relevant to her based on her age and gender, and that message will be different from what Ed Lopez, forty-six-year-old, Spanish-speaking man in the same plan, will receive. And if a participant is already doing well in one or more of the "next best step" areas, then it's not really a next best step for *them*, so they won't get the pieces of the campaign geared toward that step.

Let's say, for example, that Ed is already contributing 12% of his eligible pay to retirement – he won't get the campaign materials urging him to save more, because we know he's already in a good place with regard to saving. Because of its precision insight and targeted messaging, MassMutual's national campaign has seen a 31% increase in response rate and a 16% increase in savings from 2013 to 2014 alone.[44] Those numbers might not seem that high, but in comparison with the average direct mail response rate of 4.4%, they're significant.[45]

---

[43] Plan Sponsor Council of America Gold award, Financial Wellness & Education—General, 2013. MassMutual press release, 9/10/2013. http://www.psca.org/2013-signature-awards-winners

[44] MassMutual, "2014 RetireSmart Save: Results and Trends," unpublished/internal, 2014

[45] http://www.actiongraphicsnj.com/2014/02/25/direct-mail-is-more-effective-than-you-think/

Age-based segmentation, with an eye toward different sets of generational needs, becomes especially important as more and more Millennials come into adulthood. Traditionally, retirement communications have been focused on Baby Boomers – they're the first generation of 401(k) savers, the first since the idea of "retirement" as we know it really took hold, who likely *aren't* getting the private pension and the "golden handshake" they saw their parents get. So it makes sense that the messaging for 401(k) plans has always been geared toward them. But as the Boomers start to age out of the workforce, they'll be replaced more and more by Millennials.

Millennials "are the first generation of digital natives, born in a world where Internet access and evolving mobile technologies have shaped their life experiences," resulting in "high expectations when it comes to instant information access as well as high comfort levels with sharing information through social media."[46] Millennials' comfort with the fast-paced world of digital communication is juxtaposed with their caution when it comes to investing, a conservative mindset reminiscent of the Great Depression.

"Millennials," says Emily Pachuta, Head of Investor Insights, UBS Wealth Management Americas, "seem to be permanently scarred by the 2008 financial crisis [...] They have a Depression-Era mindset largely because they experienced market volatility and job security issues very early in their careers, or watched their parents experience them, and it has had a significant impact on their attitudes and

[46] Broadridge Financial Solutions, Inc., "Retirement Communications: Emerging and Future Trends" white paper, 2014

behaviors."[47] In addition to seeing the 2008 recession seriously endanger their parents' portfolios, Millennials are expected to pursue higher education in order to get a job – not a bad thing in theory, but because they "have more student debt than older generations did when they were younger,"[48] Millennials may feel too busy paying down debt that's due *now* to start saving for retirement.

With Millennials making up a growing chunk of the workforce, it's this odd combination of digital savvy and fiscal conservativism that must be considered when trying both to communicate with them in general, and to help them build a portfolio with an eye toward a successful retirement. Taking generational differences into account is crucial here, because what worked to get previous generations to save in their 401(k) plans is not necessarily going to fly with the workforce of the next few decades.

It's clear that knowing the audience – just like a big-box retailer knows its customers – is crucial to delivering messaging that's relevant. What will make a message relevant depends on the person you're sending that message to, and the more information you have, the more precisely targeted your message can be. But just as the power and precision engineering of a new Tesla automobile would be useless if the car was too hard to drive, targeted, relevant messaging means nothing if it's not easy to act on.

[47] Emily Pachuta, quoted in UBS NEWS, "UBS Investory Watch Report Reveals Millennials Are as Financially Conservative as Generation Born During Great Depression," January 2014, http://www.ubs.com/us/en/wealth/news/wealth-management-americas-news.html/en/2014/01/27/ubs-investor-watch-report-reveals-millennials.html

[48] Danielle Kurtzleben, Vox, "Millennials are playing it safe, and that makes them bad investors," May 2014, http://www.vox.com/2014/5/29/5758960/millennials-are-playing-it-safe-and-that-makes-them-bad-investors

Ease of action – the "just drive" ideal – is the second half of the equation. Behavioral finance tells us that different people have different comfort levels and communication preferences, so one of the best ways to get people to take action is by providing an array of contact options and letting the participants choose the way that's easiest and most convenient for them. For some, this might be over the Web. Others require a more personal touch, which is where in-person meetings and the call center come in. Indeed, some of our best results have been through personal interaction, where the teams we have in place make it easy for participants to take action.

One of these teams is made up of the MassMutual Retirement Education Specialists. The Education Specialists go through a rigorous 12-week training program upon hire, and their sole focus is to be out there in front of participants every day, helping them to understand and navigate what can be the overwhelming process of enrolling and taking action in their retirement plan. While some providers consider live educational sessions an expense they'd prefer to minimize, we see them as an investment in plan health, which is why we have roughly one hundred salaried Education Specialists on staff. This investment in plan health seems to be paying off in spades.

As a result of group meetings led by an Education Specialist, about 42% of participants take action. In one-on-one meetings, the action rate is even better at over 74%. Why? Customization again. By and large, employees already know they should be saving for retirement. But let's say an Education Specialist meets with a person who is saving 3% and they need to be saving 8%. If the Education Specialist said "you need to start saving 8%," what's the participant likely to do? Immediately more than double their contributions, or balk and list all the reasons why an increase like that is completely impossible for them?

But in a one-on-one meeting, the Education Specialist can customize the message, going even deeper than persona and addressing the needs of the person right in front of them. So rather than a flat statement of "you need to change your contributions to X percent," the conversation becomes "What do you think you can save today?" – even a small increase of 1 or 2% is a good start, and the participant can make that change right then and there in the meeting – and then, following that, "How can you get to the level of saving that will make you more likely to have adequate replacement income in retirement?" In one-on-one meetings the Education Specialist can identify and address each person's needs and concerns, and the messaging and action plan can be tailored to the individual.

This is also true when a participant contacts our call center. Although the meeting isn't physically in person, the same rule applies – the retirement professionals in the call center can customize the discussion and make sure the caller's specific needs, including taking action, are met during the call.

The e4^{SM} (enhanced electronic education experience) system is another way to personalize and customize participant interaction. In an e4^{SM} meeting, each participant uses a smart device that connects directly to MassMutual's record-keeping system. Each sees his or her retirement account information, and the touch interface allows for *immediate* action right there on the handheld rather than forcing participants to say "I really should make a change," but then having that change get lost in the shuffle when real life kicks back in. Each meeting's success in driving action is measured in real time, so employers can see right away what a difference this approach makes, not just as a general statistic but for their plan specifically. On average, e4^{SM} meetings see an 82% enrollment rate, a 50% contribution increase rate, and a 30% allocation change rate. Getting that percentage of people to do anything with regard to retirement is huge, and it's made possible because the messaging is relevant and personalized, and it's easy to take action on the spot.

Ease of action is carried through our messaging and campaigns even when a personal interaction doesn't take place. For example, the RetireSmart Ready tool pulls participants' information from the recordkeeping system and participants need only to enter four preferences; whenever there is room for improvement, the tool makes taking action as easy as clicking a button to implement the recommended change. Even on paper mailers, when action is called for, it's as simple as checking a box on the postage-paid, tear-off postcard and popping it in the mail.

Targeted messaging that's as personalized as possible gets participants' attention. Ease of action empowers them to make the changes they need to have their best chance at retiring on their own terms, with sufficient replacement income. That's what PlanALYTICS is all about.

Chapter 5:

Getting the Best into Everyone's Driveway

Who Won?

Trying to measure outcomes without all the information can be a dangerous game. Take, for example, these statistical figures from the 2015 Super Bowl.[49] Based on those numbers, who would you say won?

NEW ENGLAND		SEATTLE
25	First Downs	20
1	First Downs Rushing	8
21	First Downs Passing	10
57	Rushing Yards	162
320	Yards Passing	234
377	Total Yards	396
5 – 36	Penalties - Yards	7 – 70

Despite what the numbers seem to say, if you said Seattle, you'd be wrong – and surprising as it may be, the statistical conundrum shown here mirrors an interesting fact about how things have historically been measured in the retirement plans world.

Imagine trying to determine how each employee in a retirement plan is doing when it comes to retiring on their own terms by looking solely at activity-based measures, i.e., statistics. It would be nearly impossible. For over thirty years, since the inception of 401(k) plans, measuring activities has been the norm: How many employees have signed up for the plan? What is the average savings rate?

[49] NFL Game Center, http://www.nfl.com/gamecenter/2015020100/2014/POST22/patriots@seahawks#menu=gameinfo|contentId%3A0ap3000000468198&tab=analyze

Which investments are being utilized most and how are they performing? All of these are interesting, but none of them can tell you how much replacement income an individual will have in retirement. These measures have been thought of as real results, but they're not telling the whole story and they don't deliver the final picture – just like trying to guess who won the Super Bowl by looking at every stat but the one that really counts: the score.

Of course, there's a good reason why the focus has been, for so long, on activity-based measures – until recently, that's all we could measure. Imagine early computers, filling up whole rooms with hardware. Forget about i7 processors; vacuum tubes were the first invention that drove the processing of the smallest amounts of data possible. While the first personal computers of the 1980s were revolutionary for their time, by today's standards they would be found laughable. The limitations of computing's infancy leaned heavily on all industries including the new and budding 401(k) business, only allowing the industry to measure the activities around the edges of the plan. The algorithmic or processing "horsepower" to master the more complex simulations that are needed to truly know the score of the 401(k) – whether a person would actually be able to live in retirement – didn't exist.

The Importance of Intersections, the Power of "Why"

In *The Medici Effect: What Elephants and Epidemics Can Teach Us About Innovation*, author Frans Johansson posits that true breakthroughs come at the intersection of multiple fields of study when knowledge is blended in new combinations.[50] Johansson writes of "the movement of people, the convergence of science, and the leap of computation" that rapidly change our world for the better.

MassMutual is creating that intersection in the retirement plans world. We've got the tools: Big Data, more complex algorithms, better technology, and behavioral finance. The combination and effective use of these elements is what powers the MassMutual PlanALYTICS philosophy. But in addition to the tools, and just as important, there's the reason, the thing that motivates us – the "why."

MassMutual's "why" is to help working Americans retire on their own terms. This conviction is the keystone of our culture, and it's what drives everything we do. MassMutual PlanALYTICS is powered by that belief, and it's what allows for improvements in retirement plan measurement and design that result in more Americans having the capability to retire on their own terms.

So, just what is PlanALYTICS?

MassMutual's PlanALYTICS is a philosophy – a value system – intended to revolutionize how retirement plans work, both for the employers designing the plans and for the employees in them. Put simply, PlanALYTICS suggests that we should set a standard for how to look at plan health. This standard is built around using precision measurement to deliver insight relevant to each plan, as well as prescriptive solutions to fix whatever might be ailing that plan.

---

[50] Frans Johansson, The Medici Effect: *What Elephants and Epidemics Can Teach Us About Innovation,* Harvard Business School Press, 2006.

PlanALYTICS sets the bar for measuring and improving retirement plan health at a new high, but it's not out of reach. In fact, employers should be demanding nothing less.

How It Works

PlanALYTICS shifts the paradigm, moving measurement away from activities and toward outcomes; it sets a standard for how to measure those outcomes – a standard that combines precision engineering with "just drive" ease of action to maximize plan health. PlanALYTICS allows us to build tools to see not just how many people are enrolled in a plan, but what each participant's retirement is expected to look like. Knowing that allows us to spot opportunities and make improvements to increase everyone's chances for a better retirement.

The PlanALYTICS philosophy takes its cue, in part, from the field of genomics. When studying DNA, data is essential. To understand the strand, you have to have every part of the DNA – you can't fill in holes with estimates or assumptions, since every DNA strand is unique. It's the same with an individual's retirement savings needs – no two are exactly the same because a plan's makeup, health, and needs depend on so many different factors. In order to get precision insight and build relevant, prescriptive solutions to improve a plan's health, you need all the information about that particular plan. That's the core of the PlanALYTICS philosophy.

Remember the old way to measure retirement plan effectiveness? Compare that to the PlanALYTICS way:

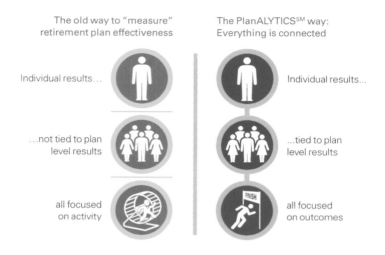

The old way to "measure" retirement plan effectiveness		The PlanALYTICS℠ way: Everything is connected
Individual results…		Individual results…
…not tied to plan level results		…tied to plan level results
all focused on activity		all focused on outcomes

Starting at the bottom: knowing the score

Many people just don't have a firm grasp on the level of financial literacy needed to direct their own investments, and behavioral finance tells us that an overwhelmed or confused person will likely give up. The PlanALYTICS philosophy connects simplicity with computational power, allowing us to make it easy for people to know where they stand with regard to replacement income in retirement. Participants have access to all this information in the easy-to-use Mass-Mutual RetireSmart Ready tool.

The RetireSmart Ready tool is just one way we're bringing the PlanALYTICS philosophy to life. It comes pre-populated with as much data, mined from modern systems, about an individual's situation as possible – that's the precision part. To start using the tool, the participant has to weigh in on just four things: desired age of retirement, replacement income percentage goal, tolerance for risk, and the percentage he or she wants to save each month. The RetireSmart Ready tool does the rest, automatically providing guidance to improve the participant's projected outcome.

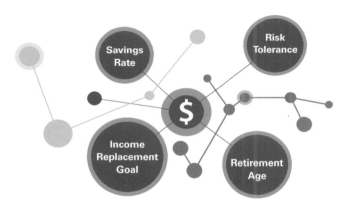

And the system is flexible – it allows users to not only state their preferences but to prioritize them. If, for example, a participant would like to retire at 65 but it's more important to him to have a higher amount of replacement income, the tool will factor that into its calculations, and will show the participant how likely he is to meet his retirement goals while following his current strategy.

Let's say a participant decides that she's not happy with what the tool tells her – for example, she only has a 60% chance of meeting her retirement goals. She wants to see what saving a little more, working a little longer, or changing her portfolio's investment risk could do to help her meet her goals. The RetireSmart Ready tool's simple interface allows her to reprioritize her preferences and immediately see what happens to her chances of success. The participant's stated preferences work in concert with each other, and the RetireSmart Ready tool is smart enough to catch preferences that are statistically improbable – say, a twenty-nine-year-old wanting to retire at forty – and offers changes to the stated preferences to deliver a solid, realistic prediction and recommendation.

Best of all, the process only takes a couple of minutes. All the complexity and sophistication of our precision engine hum along in the background, but the users don't have to worry about any of that in order to use the tool – they just have to get in and drive. With the click of a button, technology goes to work. Thousands of simulations – based on real data, not assumptions – take place behind the scenes. This processing, known as Monte Carlo simulations, seeks just one answer – is the individual on track to meet his or her goals for replacement income in retirement, or not? – and that answer is delivered in seconds.

YOUR RETIREMENT STRATEGY

Your Projected Outcomes	**Your Current Strategy**	**Chance of Sustaining Income Throughout Retirement**
Retirement Age	Age 62	
Income Replaced during Retirement	90%	
Your Action Plan		64% CURRENT CHANCE
Savings Rate	10% of salary	
Investment Portfolio	Current allocation: (29% loss potential*)	
Probability of Success	64%	

* Loss potential is the size of loss in a very bad year defined as a 2% chance of a once-in-fifty-years occurrence.

The person in the example above wants to retire at age sixty-two with 90% replacement income. Right now, there's a 64% chance of achieving that goal with current savings rates and investment selection. This is great information, and can go a long way toward helping participants get a concrete idea of where they stand in relation to their retirement goals.

But it doesn't stop here – applying PlanALYTICS to this tool allows us to go one step farther. Alongside one's current strategy, the RetireSmart Ready tool shows a recommended strategy, based on the available data, which will maximize the individual's probability of success.

In the case of this example, with a slight change in savings rate and a more moderate level of risk in the overall portfolio of investments, the probability of success can be increased to 75%. Using the "Go to What-If" button, the user can adjust her priorities until she's happy with the projection. For example, if the participant follows the tool's suggestions for bumping up contributions just a little bit (in this case, from 10% to 12%) and tweaking her asset allocation strategy, her chance of success would more than likely greatly increase.

YOUR RETIREMENT STRATEGY

Your Projected Outcomes	Your Current Strategy	Suggested Strategy	Chance of Sustaining Income Throughout Retirement
Retirement Age	Age 62	Age 62	
Income Replaced during Retirement	90%	90%	
Your Action Plan			
Savings Rate	10% of salary	12% of salary	
Investment Portfolio	Current allocation: (29% loss potential*)	Moderate (22% loss potential*)	
Probability of Success	64%	75%	

75% SUGGESTED CHANCE

64% CURRENT CHANCE

Within the application the user can click "Take Action" to adopt the Suggested Strategy or make savings and investment changes. Use "What-if" to see the impact of changing your goals.

- On target even if investments performed far worse than projected.
- On target even if investments perform worse than projected.
- On target if investmets perform as projected.
- On target only if investmets perform better than projected.
- On target only if investments perform far better than prjected.

* Loss potential is the size of loss in a very bad year defined as a 2% chance of a once-in-fifty-years occurrence.

Great, you say, but now I have to make all these changes based on the recommended strategy. Well, yes…and no. The RetireSmart Ready tool makes that easy, too: with just one click of the "Take Action" button, the participant can adopt recommended strategy and immediately get started down the road to a retirement on his or her own terms.

It really is that easy. It's the power of committing to the philosophy that allows us to drive a smarter design of retirement plan services and tools. It's the power of PlanALYTICS.

PlanALYTICS Across Channels

The power and simplicity of PlanALYTICS is that it is delivered across all participant touchpoints. This means that the information doesn't just live online in the RetireSmart Ready tool – it's scaled across the participant's whole experience: online, in direct and e-mail marketing campaigns, in one-on-one guidance sessions in person or through our call center, and on defined contribution quarterly statements. Behavioral finance tells us that easy is best, so this consistent approach – keeping the message uniform across all lines of communication – makes it easy for employees to understand, and is the most effective way to get them to take action.

That's what PlanALYTICS, through the RetireSmart Ready tool and other mediums, does for individual participants. But what about plan sponsors and their plan advisors?

Building Up to the Aggregate View

PlanALYTICS looks at the likelihood of each individual employee in a retirement plan to enjoy sufficient replacement income in his or her life after work, and connects that individual projection to the aggregate results of all the employees in that plan, so the employer can really see what is happening. This clear line of sight into the aggregate results of all employees in a plan is vital to the proper measurement of the retirement plan as a whole and to determining whether the current plan design is working for the employees participating. This is the most accurate, most precise way to measure plan health. This is what PlanALYTICS enables.

If one individual's results take thousands of Monte Carlo simulations to complete, aggregating all the results takes hundreds of thousands. That much information floating around can be confusing, but MassMutual's PlanSmart Analysisᴿᴹ takes all these transactions and provides a clean, easy-to-understand graphic view of whether a retirement plan is working. This graphic shows the percentage of employees likely to meet their retirement goals as well as the percentage that could be on target if each person were to move to his or her suggested strategy.

PlanALYTICS aggregate sponsor view: Percent of employees on target to replace at least 75% of income by age 67

This output represents a new standard for clarity, utility, and ease in retirement plan measurement: for the first time, plan sponsors and advisors can actually see if the plan is working. While many providers have a plan health score, chart, graph, or image, only MassMutual's has the precision and ease of action driven by the PlanALYTICS philosophy.

And if you think of the PlanALYTICS retirement plan as a highly sophisticated engine driving the retirement car, there's a bonus in the trunk for plan sponsors. Financial stress is a problem for almost everyone, to some degree; in April 2014, the PricewaterhouseCoopers Employee Financial Wellness Survey showed that 24% of employees (nearly one in four) report that personal finance issues have been a distraction at work. If employees' financial issues encroach on work enough to affect performance, it can also affect the employer's costs. "These 'lost hours' can really add up and have a significant impact on an employer's bottom line. Increased stress levels also may lead to higher health care costs and impact morale" – all problems which can be largely nipped in the bud with a smart plan design based on the PlanALYTICS philosophy.

PlanALYTICS Helps Everyone: Employees, Employers, and Advisors

The power and simplicity of PlanALYTICS aren't limited to just helping the participants on an individual level – it helps everyone involved in the retirement plan.

Advisors and third-party administrators can show the value they provide to the plan by using our Prescriptive Solutions to make plan design and participant campaign suggestions based on real data. Down the road, they can use the PlanSmart Analysis tool to demonstrate the increased effectiveness of tailored plan design and participant action programs. The PlanALYTICS philosophy and its associated tools and measures allow advisors to have deeper, richer conversations about a plan's health. The tools can help advisors show where a plan is and where it could be, and the advisor can recommend the best changes for that plan's specific needs, strengthening the advisor's relationship with the plan and helping the plan to grow. In addition, the tools enable the advisor to measure his or her own effectiveness – positive movement toward higher retirement readiness scores proves the value that the advisor has contributed to the plan during the year.

Sponsors, too, have plenty to gain from engaging with the PlanALYTICS philosophy. Precise measurement allows VPs of human resources to demonstrate to CEOs and CFOs the value the plan is driving and how it supports their talent acquisition and retention strategies. Measuring plan performance and seeing progress is a good way to hold the advisor accountable for his or her work with the plan. All this information enables plan sponsors to evaluate plan effectiveness based on real information – not assumptions – and to make any adjustments necessary to fulfill their fiduciary duty.

There's a beauty in the symbiosis here: when plan sponsors know what's working and what's not, they can adjust their plan design to better meet participants' needs; in return, whether intentional or not, financially well employees who are enabled by their employer to retire on their own terms are simply more productive. It's a win for everyone, and that's part of the beauty of the PlanALYTICS philosophy.

You've already seen how behind-the-scenes precision allows for prescriptive recommendations, and how all of that power is bundled into a user-friendly package for ease of action. But just as a philosophy is only as good as the actions taken to support it, a plan is only as healthy as the actions its participants are taking toward saving for their retirement. The more solid participation a plan has, the better its health will be. With that in mind, let's take a look at how the PlanALYTICS philosophy is geared toward driving participants to take action in their retirement plans and challenging the idea of a retirement crisis in America.

Chapter 6:

The Checkered Flag

Precision insight and ease of action are at the core of getting participants engaged in saving for retirement, but you can't just throw precision and action out into the world and claim victory. The only way to really gauge the success of all that precision and ease of action is to measure the results, so MassMutual has done just that. Based on the measurement, it's clear that PlanALYTICS makes a positive difference. Let's look at the data at three levels: plans using our Prescriptive Solutions, PlanSmart^{SM} Analysis, and RetireSmart Ready tools, those plans against the overall book of business, and case studies of individual client successes.

The Power of Prescriptive Solutions

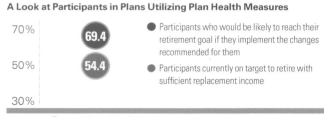

A Look at Participants in Plans Utilizing Plan Health Measures

December 31, 2014

The table above shows two corresponding levels of participant retirement readiness for participants on the Mass-Mutual system. The red point represents participants in plans using the PlanALYTICS plan health measures who are expected to retire with sufficient income using their current contributions and investment strategy, while the green point shows the higher percent who are likely to reach their retirement goal if they implement the changes recommended for them. It's clear that the percentage of participants likely to be able to retire on their own terms is higher when the PlanALYTICS plan health suggestions are implemented.

Comparing Plans Using PlanSMART Analysis and RetireSmart[SM] Ready to the Overall Client Base

Let's take another view of the results – comparing just the MassMutual clients who are using the most sophisticated PlanALYTICS tools we offer to the entire book of business. For clients participating in the plan health program, getting to review a detailed analysis of their plan's health and receiving prescriptive recommendations for improvement are a matter of course, and it's clear that those plans are doing better as a result.

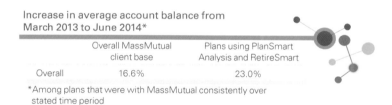

Increase in average account balance from March 2013 to June 2014*		
	Overall MassMutual client base	Plans using PlanSmart Analysis and RetireSmart
Overall	16.6%	23.0%

*Among plans that were with MassMutual consistently over stated time period

One additional interesting fact is that when this data is cut by gender, rather than age, a sharp contrast emerges. Female plan health participants show a 38.87% increase in their account balances and an 18.75% increase in deferrals; their male counterparts show 22.72% and 7.89% increases respectively. While the outcomes for men are strong and outpace the control group results, they lag significantly behind the women's results.

We credit such great success to three things: the fact that our precision measurement of data allows us to paint a clear picture of where a person is now with their savings and where they could or should be, the fact that we make it easy to make those changes, and the fact that we factor gender into our personas, delivering targeted, relevant messaging and images. Together, these three things drive improved outcomes for plans and their participants.

Plan Health Improvement through PlanALYTICS : Three Success Stories

That's a general look at how PlanALYTICS affects overall plan health on the books, but what about more specific client examples? How are real-life plans[51] seeing real improvement through implementing strategies based in the PlanALYTICS philosophy?

Profile of Success #1

Client #1 is an engineering and environmental sciences firm with more than 900 eligible employees. They have 22 locations nationwide and have been with MassMutual since 1985. In 2006, their "traditional" plan metrics appeared quite average – 5% deferral rate and 65% participation rate. MassMutual's PlanSmart^{SM} Analysis report added a new dimension to the reporting, showing that only 32% of their employees were on track to replace 75% of their income at retirement. This insight contributed to the company's motivation to adopt the prescriptive solutions to (1) redesign their plan to include automatic enrollment and automatic deferral increase features and (2) deliver a targeted employee

---

[51] Plan names are omitted to protect privacy.

communication campaign that included mailings and live meetings.

This client's history of working with MassMutual afforded an excellent opportunity for measurement over time, and the results are staggering.

Client #1's plan metrics from Jan. 2006 to June 2014

	Jan-06	Jun-14	Increase
Average savings rate	5.0%	7.9%	58.0%
Plan participation rate	65.0%	96.0%	47.7%
Participants prepared to retire	32.0%	68.0%	112.5%
Total assets	$49.5m	$151m	205%

Between 2006 and 2014 all of the measures increased; most notable was the increase in participants prepared to retire, which more than doubled: going from 32% in 2006 to 68% in 2014.

That single change in plan design, paired with targeted messaging, was able to more than double the number of their employees on track for a comfortable retirement. With the research that links financial stress to productivity, one can only imagine the positive domino effect that this could have on the company's business results. For this client, the tools and solutions that embody the PlanALYTICS philosophy are making material differences in improving plan health and helping working Americans retire on their own terms.

Profile of Success #2

Client #2 operates multiple racetracks and casinos around the country, and also has a hand in online gaming. At the time this profile was created, the company had 3,985 eligible but unenrolled employees in eight locations across America, many of them paid hourly and employed on a seasonal basis. As you can imagine, those conditions make it more difficult to motivate people to save for the long term. The company asked MassMutual for help. Specifically, they wanted to focus on these unenrolled employees and increase:

1. employees' awareness of their retirement plan options;

2. the participation rate (27.82% in the plan overall, with 0% participation in the target group) and

3. employee deferral rates.

Plan design changes were not practical for this client, so they went after the improvements that could be garnered through a targeted employee campaign. The campaign targeted 3,450 employees – in and of itself accomplishing objective number one in creating broader awareness of the plan. It included a series of on-site and online education meetings and two print pieces that were mailed to employees' homes. More than 550 employees attended the on-site and online meetings.

Of those at the meetings, an overwhelming 74% of attendees took action and either enrolled in the plan or increased their savings rate. We've already seen the techniques that MassMutual's Retirement Education Specialists employ to effectively motivate and make it easy to take action in the moment at meetings and e4^{SM} sessions. These results demonstrate how powerful it can be when those techniques are put into practice.

As for the mail components, both used simple tear-off reply cards to drive action and both achieved industry norm response rates of 2.3% and 1.97%. Collectively, as a result of both the mailers and the meetings, this client increased their plan participation by 10.6% with the new enrollees deferring on average 5.32% of their wages. Persona-based marketing and ease of action came through in helping to deliver above-par results.

Profile of Success #3

Client #3 is a business with just over 300 employees, a force composed of both manufacturing workers and corporate staff. In early 2012, during a plan and investment review, MassMutual and the plan advisor introduced this client to the PlanSmart[SM] Analysis Report. It was the first time they had seen retirement readiness outcome data – a plan health score – that moved beyond average participation rates, deferral rates, and account balances. Knowing that only 24% of their employees were prepared to retire with at least a 75% replacement income ratio motivated them to action.

In partnership with the plan's advisor, MassMutual delivered prescriptive solutions that spanned both plan design improvements and targeted participant campaigns. On the plan design side, the client added automatic enrollment and automatic deferral increase features. They then held thirty employee meetings over two days, accommodating the schedules of both first- and second-shift workers.

How effective were these meetings? Did they justify pulling people out of production? Again, the data tells the story. An incredible 82% of those who attended a meeting took positive action in their plan. The result: average deferral rates increased by 2.4%. Even more importantly, the company saw an incredible 70.8% increase in the plan's health – from this one effort alone, the plan's original 24% employee readiness rate climbed to 41% likely to retire with sufficient replacement income.

Plan successes like these are staggering, especially since getting a room full of people to take action on their retirement plan is a monumental feat. The key to driving that action is the key to PlanALYTICS – comprehensive data allows precision; precision powers targeted messaging; and targeted messaging combined with ease of action drive engagement, dramatically increasing the chances of getting participants involved in their retirement plan. Both the overall data and specific success stories show that plans that follow these steps – the basic steps in the PlanALYTICS philosophy – are doing better than the overall book of business. Precision and action drive positive, measurable results and empower more working Americans to retire on their own terms.

Chapter 7:

What's Next – Flying Cars?

Helping retirement plans to achieve success and increase their employees' retirement readiness is what PlanALYTICS is all about. But the status quo is in a state of flux even now. Consumers receive increasingly tailored retail advertisements that lure their minds and money away from saving for the future, while the benefits landscape is at the start of a major shift that will profoundly affect how participants take part in the selection of their whole benefits package. We need to find a way to keep customers engaged and informed, so that we can continue to help them meet the challenges that lie ahead and stay focused on saving for the future.

Personas of the Future: RetireSmart^{SM} ***GENERATIONS***

Tailoring retirement plan messaging based on age and gender is a powerful tool in getting participants to take notice and take action, but in the grand scheme of things, generational marketing isn't enough. After all, as social media strategist Drew Hubbard states,

> …[T]he goal of defining generations has typically been to identify groups of people with shared experiences. That might have had some merit a few decades back when media was so limited and controlled that people truly did seem to share only the experiences that made headlines – wars, presidential elections, national tragedies, etc. But today – and arguably for some time

now – we have media, news, and culture
coming out of our ears. *Everything* is a
shared experience.[52]

Hubbard also argues that "age groups simply don't equate to life stages anymore […] lots of people are waiting longer and longer to have children [and] not everyone in the expected generation is retiring when conventions say they should."[53]

The changing face and greater connectedness of our society call for more refinement in the way we reach out. Specification and personalization are critical to getting through to a participant – this has always been more or less the case, but with the increasing flexibility in combinations of age and life stage, it rises to the top of the priorities list.

Consider, if you will, two random fifty-five-year-olds: people who would generally be categorized as "pre-retiree." One of them is two years away from retirement, and is going to need help making the transition and figuring out how to withdraw and spend the money they've been accumulating for so long. Messaging surrounding those topics, the classic pre-retiree fare, would be appropriate for that person. But the other fifty-five-year-old, far from retiring, has a child in high school. For someone whose immediate concern is putting their kid through college, messages saying "we see you're close to retirement" aren't going to cut it, because they're probably *not* close to retirement, and because that participant would be at risk for feeling that his or her provider doesn't have any idea what's going on, so how could

[52] Drew Hubbard, "Why generational marketing is ridiculous," October 2013, http://www.imediaconnection.com/content/35038.asp#singleview
[53] Ibid.

they possibly be relied on for something as important as retirement planning?

With all that in mind, MassMutual's next step for further segmentation lies in the forthcoming RetireSmart **GENERATIONS** program. RetireSmart **GENERATIONS** will take the age and gender information used in today's personas and layer it with a person's life stage or lifestyle – whether they're single, married without children, young families, or established families, all the way up to empty nesters. This will allow the messaging that participants receive to be more relevant to *them* – not just to generic expectations for their age group or their gender, but to them personally, and that kind of tailored message will increase the chances of that participant taking action.

In order to achieve maximum efficacy, the future of persona-based marketing must involve a personalized experience for each customer, a complete 180 from the one-size-fits-all approach that marketing has taken for so long. Take a look at the difference better segmentation can make:

Segmentation + Personalization = Greater Results

	Phase 1 1 Segment	Phase 2 24 Segments	Phase 3 24 Segments
Segments	One segment, generalized messaging for all	Personalized imagery by age, gender, channel, language	Truly personalized and segment-specific content and imagery
Target	198,000	365,000	350,078
Response Rate	1.81%	3.79%	4.99%

Phase 1 in the chart above reflects the "spray and pray," one-size-fits-all approach. That's a good baseline to start from, because phase 2, with personalized imagery segmented by age, gender, channel, and language, boasts better results. This kind of personalization is still relatively general; the imagery and age references amount to basically taking a target demographic and personalizing the materials for that demographic with a single representative image – a thirtysomething black woman, or a white man over fifty, for example. Phase 3, a step up from that, reflects a campaign phase in which materials were personalized not just with a demographic representative image, but with timeline imagery that represented significant pop-culture events starting from about when the target demographic was born – things they would have grown up with, to which they would respond instantly with memories and affinity. You can see that even with that small difference, response rates jumped again.

With those three sample phases serving as a baseline, it's easy to see how effective segmentation drives ever-increasing response rates. Now imagine what kind of responses could be achieved when taking into account things like life stage (as the Generations program intends to do) and personal attitudes toward saving. For example, the message would be different for a twentysomething male with a young family and a desire to save than it would be for his thirtysomething brother, still single and uninterested in the future. Taking every possible element into account – from age to attitude and everything in between – allows us to move marketing from one-size-fits-all to one-size-fits-one. Getting as close as we can to a one-to-one marketing approach is the ideal state, because the more relevant we can make our messaging for each individual, especially in the changing face of today's workforce as Boomers begin to age into retirement, the more likely a participant is to take action and start saving adequately for a retirement on their own terms.

A Word on the Future of Employee Benefits

It is absolutely clear that the shift from traditional defined benefit pension plans to the defined contribution savings and investment model has meant significant changes in the way we reach and provide for retirement, but the retirement savings landscape isn't the only one that's changing. Benefits, too, seem to be shifting, partly due to the Patient Protection and Affordable Care Act (PPACA), which has "precipitated a new appreciation for voluntary benefits." [54]

Benefits seem almost to be following in the footsteps of retirement's evolution. Consider this: traditional defined benefit pensions, which guarantee a certain payout at retirement, were once the norm. When ERISA came along, it

> had an effect on traditional pension plans
> and killed some of them, [and changes in
> ERISA regulations over time] have caused
> significant problems for employers both
> with financial statements and funding re-
> sponsibilities that would not have occurred
> with the old rules and the old ways of
> investing… [These problems have] caused
> employers to move away from defined

[54] Heather Lavallee, "Employee Benefits: It's time to tell a new story," http://www.life-healthpro.com/2014/10/09/employee-benefits-its-time-to-tell-a-new-story; hereinafter cited as 'Heather Lavallee, "Employee Benefits"'

benefit plans and the volatility involved with
funding them and to shift both the cost and
risk for retirement benefits to employees.[55]

When maintaining defined benefits became too problematic for employers, the majority bowed out of providing pension income in retirement. However, they couldn't just leave employees completely on their own; hence, the advent of the defined contribution plan, which puts the onus for savings and investing, outside of employer contributions, mainly on each individual saver.

Benefits beyond the retirement plan – things like life, health, and disability insurance – seem to be starting down that road as well, moving toward a defined contribution-style approach and placing more responsibility for benefits selection on employees, rather than employers. "Businesses," says Heather Lavallee, president of the Employee Benefits business at Voya Financial, Inc. (formerly ING U.S.), "are enhancing their benefits packages to offset rising healthcare costs and to allow employees to fill the gaps left behind by high-deductible health plans." [56]

Employees will increasingly be held accountable for selecting and paying for their own benefits, so it's up to providers, advisors, and plan sponsors to make sure employees are informed and able to make the decisions that best suit their needs. Just as in persona-based marketing, people's preferences, attitudes, and lifestyles all come into play here.

---

[55] James van Iwaarden, consulting actuary with Minneapolis-based Van Iwaarden Associates, quoted by Lisa Beyer in "The Rise and Fall of Employer-Sponsored Pension Plans," *Workforce.com,* January 2012, http://www.workforce.com/articles/the-rise-and-fall-of-employer-sponsored-pension-plans

[56] Heather Lavallee, "Employee Benefits"

One person might need to focus on retirement savings first, while another might need to worry more about providing for a long-term disability. A lot depends on the individual. There's also that Millennial mentality growing in the workforce: "The next generation of employees expects coverage options that enhance their work-life balance, improve their overall quality of life, and safeguard their financial future."[57]

The key here is that involving participants in the selection of their benefits, much as they select how to invest in their 401(k), allows a more holistic approach to benefits in general. The focus here isn't just on retirement savings; it widens the lens with a broadened perspective and wants to find the most appropriate and maximized portfolio of worksite benefits, of which traditional retirement savings is just one. As participant involvement in selection of benefits – from health insurance to retirement and everything in between – grows deeper, so does the challenge of figuring out how to do this well. When just talking about retirement alone, the issues of technical complexity and affordability are barriers to many people. Throw health care and insurance benefits into the mix, and it has the potential to become paralyzing.

MassMutual aims to meet this need through our forthcoming worksite solutions program, MassMutual@**WORK**^{SM}. It offers one centralized place to get information on all types of insurance an employee might need, and insurance offered through the workplace tends to be perceived more favorably.[58] In addition, there's the same ease as with retirement contributions – they can come directly out of the paycheck,

[57] Ibid.
[58] MassMutual Worksite VOC (Voice of the Customer) study, 2014

so there's no need to remember to write a check or pay a bill.

Benefits aren't just important for employees; a good benefits package can have a profound effect on employers as well, because in "the race for qualified candidates, a well-designed benefits package will become increasingly useful for employers in recruiting and retaining top talent."[59] So how do we get employees to engage in the selection of benefits, a task which has always been left up to the employer? According to Lavallee, it's as simple as changing the story. "It goes without saying," she says,

> that a life-threatening health event can have a profound negative impact on a family's financial well-being, but even a short-term illness or injury can derail one's retirement readiness. To demonstrate that point, we need to present common, real-life situations that can help make products like disability income, critical illness, and accident insurance more than just theoretical concepts. By demystifying these products, and presenting them as the solution to a problem, we're able to tell a new story — one that positions employee benefits as an important part of every American's overall retirement readiness strategy.[60]

Benefits planning will become increasingly important not just for its own sake but as a part of protecting retirement savings as well. MassMutual is committed to helping

[59] Heather Lavallee, "Employee Benefits"
[60] Ibid.

our participants achieve as much security as possible in all aspects of retirement readiness, and worksite benefits are becoming more and more a part of that picture.

As that happens, it's imperative that employees are not just involved but *informed*, and able to make good choices. Putting the responsibility for benefits selection and purchasing on the employee makes things somewhat easier for employers, but it presents new challenges for both groups. Employers now have to get their employees involved in the benefits process, and employees have to be able to understand what's going on so they can make informed, appropriate decisions. MassMutual's Voice of the Customer research[61] on the subject found that overall, people find insurance and benefits to be "confusing, frustrating, and even overwhelming."[62] It doesn't do them much good to have a tablefull of options if they have no idea where to start, so two things become important during a transition to employee-selected benefits.

The first is clear communication. Employees responsible for selecting their own benefits want "clear language,"[63] not a bunch of confusing insurance jargon that will leave them wondering if they're even choosing the right thing at all. Lavallee recommends this as well, charging insurance providers to

> talk about employee benefits *in a way that [is] clear and understandable to the lay person, not just those who live and breathe insurance.* For a moment, let's forget about

[61] MassMutual Worksite VoC (Voice of the Customer) study, 2014
[62] MassMutual Worksite VOC (Voice of the Customer) study, 2014
[63] Ibid.

premiums, terms, and disclosures and talk about what these products were created to do, which is assist individuals in meeting monthly expenses in the wake of an illness or injury, thus helping them protect their retirement savings and remain on track to achieve their financial goals.[64]

Clarity of language needs to be paired with the second thing: clarity of choice, or a way to help employees narrow down the selections and end up with what's right for them. Precision engineering and prescriptive recommendations can once again come in handy in the building of tools that help employees take stock of their own personal situation and fill their basket with the benefits combination that's exactly right for them.

Allowing employees to tailor their insurance and benefits so that they're getting exactly the coverage they need and not paying for coverage they don't need is great, but employers who go down this road need to make sure that their employees are clearly, usefully informed. This will allow them to select exactly the benefits mix that's right for them, and will help them to align their benefits needs with their overall financial strategy to best protect not only their health but their finances and retirement as well.

MassMutual is meeting the growing trend of defined-contribution-style benefits with the 2015 launch of the MassMutual@**WORK**SM program. This solution set includes portable insurance products, administration services, and the MapMy**BENEFITS**SM guidance tool for employees. This

[64] Heather Lavallee, "Employee Benefits," italics added for emphasis

program will guide participants – in fifteen minutes or less – to the most appropriate portfolio of benefits for them. Retirement savings is, of course, one of those benefits, but other benefits like life, health, and disability insurance will be brought into play as well, and recommendations will be made based on a person's lifestyle, needs, and other factors.

Participants will be presented with the optimal suite of benefits for their particular situation, but they'll also get alternate recommendations for what might be more *affordable*, so they'll have options available to further tailor their benefits to exactly what fits their budget, lifestyle, and needs.

MapMy**BENEFITS**^{SM} is revolutionary for three reasons. First, the integration and prioritization of benefits decision making for health care, insurance, and retirement into one place mean that people can take a whole look at their options across the span from health care to retirement and see what the best fit is for them overall. Second, the tool takes affordability into account – by knowing your salary and family situation, the tool can recommend a suite of benefits that balances affordability with your personal needs. Third, it's easy to use. MapMy**BENEFITS**^{SM} uses the PlanALYTICS principle of a precision engine behind the scenes that makes it easy and quick for the employer to use. This holistic approach combines retirement readiness with readiness for anything else that might come a person's way before they reach that milestone, and allows participants the flexibility to retire on their own terms and take the appropriate steps to protect the ones that matter most to them.

Closing Thoughts

 S ince the decline of the defined benefit plan, the defined contribution model has borne a lot of criticism. To begin, it's important to recognize that the 401(k) and other savings vehicles like it were originally intended to be just one of multiple sources of retirement income, supplementing things like Social Security and personal savings. It was never meant to carry the entire weight of a person's retirement income needs.

Times change, though, and in a society where the sustainability of Social Security faces its own challenges and personal long-term savings outside the 401(k) seem to be largely a thing of the past, it's natural for eyes and fingers to start pointing at the 401(k), expecting it to save the day and slinging criticism when it can't instantly do so for every American. And no, the 401(k) *can't* instantly save every American's retirement, but the important thing to remember is that it's not because the model itself doesn't work – it's either because it's not being used properly, or because our first wave of retirees with defined contribution retirement accounts never had enough time to use that vehicle as it was intended to be used.

 In fact, when used appropriately from the start of a person's working life, a defined contribution plan actually has the potential to surpass its original intent and become the major, if not the sole, source of a person's retirement income.

The Generational Lens: A Closer Look at the Defined Contribution Model

To explore this further, rather than using the entire pool of working Americans as our sample size, let's reframe the conversation and talk about savings potential by generation, starting with Generation Y, or the Millennials.

The math indicates that if a Millennial enrolls in her retirement plan at the start of her working life, allocates sensibly, and puts aside, including any company match, about ten percent of her salary over the course of forty years, she will have a very high probability of being ready when she reaches retirement.[65] This is a perfect example of the defined contribution model succeeding beyond expectations, working better than it was designed to.

One of the big differences with Millennials as compared to Generation X and the Boomers before them is their mentality. They are the first generation that, as a whole, has little to no expectation of their employer providing for their income in retirement. In fact, two-thirds of Millennials expect "to self-fund their primary source of income in retirement accounts such as 401(k)s, 403(b)s, IRAs, or other outside savings."[66] While Generation X might have had parents or grandparents with pensions, defined benefit plans were on their way out as Gen X was entering the workforce, and for the majority of Millennials, the defined benefit model is little more than a scrap of history.[67] In addition to the understanding that no one else is going to do their saving for them, Millennials compound their advantage with the benefit of a

---

[65] Example assumes an average six percent rate of return and defines readiness as being able to retire at age sixty-seven with seventy-five percent replacement income.

[66] Catherine Collinson, Transamerica Center for Retirement Studies, "The Retirement Readiness of Three Unique Generations: Baby Boomers, Generation X, and Millennials 15th Annual Transamerica Retirement Survey of Workers," April 2014, http://www.transamericacenter.org/docs/default-source/resources/center-research/tcrs2014_sr_three_unique_generations.pdf

[67] U.S. Social Security Administration Office of Retirement and Disability Policy, "The Disappearing Defined Benefit Pension and Its Potential Impact on the Retirement Incomes of Baby Boomers," http://www.ssa.gov/policy/docs/ssb/v69n3/v69n3p1.html

considerable time horizon – that is, plenty of time to build their savings in preparation for retirement – and the median age at which Millennials start saving for retirement is 22.[68]

If we continue to educate the younger generation of savers about the benefits of starting early and saving well in their defined contribution retirement plan over the course of their working lives, evidence points to the strong likelihood that they will reach retirement with sufficient income. The best part is that if Millennials have the time to save and retire on their 401(k), so will the generations after them. And just like that, a whole demographic of roughly 80 million Americans has the opportunity to use the 401(k) to help them retire on their own terms.[69] The biggest challenge for this generation is *access* to a 401(k) – but that's a topic for another book.

What about Generation X? Many had access to and saved in 401(k)s at the onset of their careers, and for those people, the outlook is similar to that of the Millennials who start saving as soon as they get into their plan. But some did not. For that group, the focus needs to be on education: the more we in the retirement industry can motivate Generation X to take personal action, the better their chances will be to close the gap and reach an appropriate savings level. This education and motivation can include "easy enroll" postcards, as well as e-mail campaigns with links to the websites where they can easily increase deferral rates, use calculators, and see gap statements to help them determine their next best steps. Depending on a person's individual needs and lifestyle, some of those steps might include altering savings and spending patterns or adjusting the aggressiveness of their

[68] Ibid.
[69] RetireSmart^{SM} **Generations** Program Overview, December 2014; see also www.census.gov.

allocations. Generation X might not have quite the same time-horizon advantage as the Millennials, but by and large most should still have enough time to change their habits and get at least close to where they want to be in time for retirement. Effective, high-quality application of persona-based marketing means that there's a second group of roughly 65.7 million[70] Americans who can take advantage of the 401(k) and have it work effectively for them.

Admittedly, the 75 million[71] Baby Boomers, on the whole, face a different situation. Let's loosely define the Boomers as age fifty or above, with fifteen or fewer years to retire-ment. Many Boomers may have entered the workforce with the expectation that their experience would mirror their parents' – i.e. that they didn't have to do their own saving because there was a pension floating around somewhere, or that they'd be able to rely on what used to be a much more robust Social Security payout. Boomers who didn't start saving early and continue to save over the course of their working lives can still change behaviors to make some difference, but the longer one waits to save, the more dif-ficult it will be at age sixty-seven to establish a reasonable replacement income for retirement. What is it that's working against them right now? It's not the structure of the 401(k) – it's *time.*

Because of their shorter glide path to retirement, Boom-ers need more than the quick action tools that are effective for Gen Xers. They need deeper interaction with more per-sonalized dialogue and guidance. The discussion with this group needs to be about understanding – do you under-

[70] Ibid.
[71] Ibid.

stand whether you will have sufficient replacement income? The PlanALYTICS-driven tools are a great way to furnish this understanding, working as they do with personally tailored information. And if the answer turns out to be no, I *won't* have sufficient replacement income, the focus can turn to things like catch-up contributions, working longer, deferring Social Security until age seventy, cutting expenses where possible, and looking at supplementing savings with benefits products outside the 401(k), such as critical or long-term care insurance, to protect against longevity risk.

These variables will all depend on a person's health and personal situation, and this opportunity for education is why the initial rollout of the RetireSmart **GENERATIONS** program targets pre-retirees. In an effort to generate relevant, useful dialogues, the pre-retiree program focuses on two things: gathering better information and then using that information to create customized messaging that will help pre-retirees define their goals. As a base, the RetireSmart **GENERATIONS** program uses existing data, such as third-party and voice-of-the-customer research as well as common events that affect the financial health and well-being of individuals approaching retirement age. The initial rollout includes increased touchpoints in a 12-month e-mail campaign, as well as customized webinars and invitations for a free 15-minute call with a MassMutual specialist. Through these efforts and conversations, the RetireSmart **GENERATIONS** program empowers individuals to address their oncoming retirement and take whatever action is most appropriate for their needs and situation.

The Bottom Line

Retirement has gone through many evolutions since pre-history and each evolution has been, to some extent, a sign of its times. From early Industrial America to the golden years of defined benefit pensions through to employee-funded defined contribution plans and the newly evolving benefits landscape, retirement has changed and will continue to do so as the world around it does the same. The American audience – and the things that command its attention – will evolve as the world shapes generations to come, and each new generation will, as they have in the past, demand its own methods of communication. For early savers it was simply mail, while for today's savers it is e-mails, texts, websites, and apps, and who knows what it will be thirty years from now. But however communications evolve, they'll still be centered on one core message: save early, save appropriately, and you have an excellent chance of reaching your retirement with sufficient replacement income. And for those folks who don't have enough time to save before they hit retirement, communications must be tailored to helping them make the most of their situation.

When examined through the generational lens it's clear that, when used appropriately, the defined contribution model can work and *does* work. The fear that came with the decline of the defined benefit plan and the sudden expectation of the defined contribution plan to save the day have created what we know as America's retirement crisis. But the lack of savings in some households, while unfortunate for those affected, is not a reflection of a failing 401(k) system but of expectations and lack of retirement savings education clashing with reality. Some would argue that a 401(k) or other retirement savings vehicle is all well and good for people who work a job that offers one, but express concern for low earners who don't have the means to contribute meaningfully to a retirement savings plan. But if the overall goal of retirement is to maintain one's standard of living after leaving the workforce, it's likely that Social Security will cover the needs of those low earners. And for people who do have the means to save but lack the motivation, it's often a matter of educating them to understand *why* saving for retirement is both important and achievable.

The retirement crisis is, ultimately, a crisis of understanding: when you don't understand your situation, when you're confused or overwhelmed and there's doom and gloom all around you, it can be tough to take action, to know what to do or even where to start. Fear is often the thief of reason, but if you *do* understand your situation, you're in a better position to take control of it. The outlook changes when a person's fear is removed from the discussion and replaced with awareness and understanding, both of his or her current situation and of what adjustments need to be made to bring that person as close as possible to reaching retirement with sufficient replacement income.

Whatever the future has in store, MassMutual's PlanALYTICS philosophy will allow us to rise to the challenge. We will continue to refine our use of data and plan measurement to gain precise insight into each plan's needs, and will pair that measurement with an understanding of behavioral finance to build tailored, prescriptive strategies to help plans increase their readiness for retirement. We will pay attention to the needs of our customers, combining age, gender, and lifestyle information with language and communication type preferences, ensuring that our messaging will be increasingly tailored, timely, and relevant. We will keep a holistic mindset, understanding that people's needs are driven by many factors, and that taking as much as we can into account – not just for retirement for but health care and other benefits as well – will allow us to help Americans determine the most efficient allocation of their resources across their larger financial plan. We will do all this with PlanALYTICS, which brings precision and action to plan health.

Through all the changes sure to come our way, Mass-Mutual is committed, in the end, to one thing: helping more working Americans achieve a retirement on their own terms.